SADDAM HU

C000125495

A Life From Beginning to End

Copyright © 2018 by Hourly History.

Table of Contents

Introduction

President of Iraq for more than two decades, Saddam Hussein had a knack for acquiring power. Emerging on the revolutionary political scene as a young man, Hussein made an alliance with the Ba'athist Party. On one hand, Hussein developed a reputation as a thug who had no problem using violence to achieve the party's ends; on the other, acquaintances considered him charming, articulate, and well-read. A true revolutionary, Saddam Hussein was a man of action whose seemingly open-minded approach to policy had the potential to steer Iraq into a new era. Or so it seemed.

Hussein was responsible for the nationalization of Iraqi oil and foreign banks, a move that generated great economic prosperity. He put this revenue into state welfare programs and improved the national infrastructure. Iraq established universal free schooling, a National Campaign for the Eradication of Illiteracy, support for families of soldiers, free hospitalization to all, and the most modernized public-health system in the Middle East. But the improvements to the lives of ordinary Iraqis was short-lived. The Iran-Iraq War, the Gulf War, and subsequent UN sanctions destroyed any societal benefits that trickled down from all that oil money.

The brutality of Hussein's dictatorship outweighed his utopian promise of a united Arab world. Purges within his government, genocide of minority groups, and the invasions of Iran and Kuwait lent Hussein the nickname "The Butcher of Baghdad."

Hussein was executed after the Iraqi court found him guilty of crimes against humanity, related to the 1982 killing of 148 Iraqi people. But the death toll of Saddam Hussein's reign was much higher than that. The buck stops at the top, and the Butcher of Baghdad bore responsibility for the deaths of thousands of Iraqis, Kuwaitis, Iranians, and members of coalition military forces during his reign.

Hussein grew up in an Iraq that was already cultivating the perfect conditions to create a great dictator. The Iraq he left behind is still recovering from the aftershocks of his demise.

Chapter One

Humble Origins

*"The lion does not care about a monkey laughing at him
from a tree."*

—Saddam Hussein

Saddam Hussein was born on April 28, 1937. In a public
relations stunt in 1980, Hussein would make this date a
public holiday and fund several days of public
celebrations. It's possible, however, that he was born on a
different date as no evidence of his birth exists. Hussein's
complete given name was Saddam Hussein Abd al-Majid
al-Tikriti. The al-Tikriti part of his name should refer to
the place he was born, a common Iraqi custom at the time.
Yet Hussein was not born in the town of Tikrit but in the
nearby Sunni-Muslim village of Al-Awja. Al-Awja means
"crooked," while Saddam means "one who confronts."
Had Hussein kept his actual place of birth in his name the
meaning would be "the crooked one who confronts."

Saddam's parents were Hussein Abd al-Majid and
Subha Tulfah al-Mussallat. His father, Hussein, was
missing and presumed dead before Saddam was born. The
details of his death are unclear. Popular theories assert he
either died of natural causes, was murdered by bandits, or
left in order to escape an unhappy marriage. Accounts of

Subha's personality paint her as a formidable woman. Subha took part in family meetings that were traditionally the domain of men and took liberties with the traditional *abba* she was expected to wear. Ahead of her time, Subha refused to be treated as a subordinate of her husbands.

The area in which Hussein grew up was poverty-stricken. Most of the land around Al-Awja and Tikrit was owned by the state, but no agricultural investment was ever made. As a result, the people who lived on this land were poor and disease was rife. Families survived by growing vegetables and wheat, but life was hard and opportunities were few. This was tribal land. Each small village was the domain of a clan, but Al-Bu Nasir, a tribe of Sunni Muslims, ruled the area as a whole. Hussein's clan was al-Khatab and stood out as one of the more violent and cunning Al-Bu Nasir clans. The seizing of power was every clan's main goal and the chief concern of its paternal leader. Both critics and supporters of Hussein later traced the extreme atrocities of his rule back to his clan roots. Hussein would become an al-Khatab engaging in clan warfare but on a global scale.

At the age of five, al-Khatab children, like hundreds of thousands of other village children in Iraq, were given distinctive tattoos. Boys, like Hussein, were given three dark-blue dots in a line near their wrist. Girls, like Hussein's mother, were marked by facial tattoos on their chins, foreheads, or cheeks. Many of these marked children tried to fade their tattoos with bleach when they moved to cities and improved their status. Hussein, however, never tried to remove the evidence of his humble birth, despite his claim that he was a direct descendant of the prophet Muhammad.

Soon after Hussein's birth, Subha lost her older son to cancer. Hussein's brother was 13 years old when he died and, having lost both her husband and son and given birth in a short space of time, Subha was overwhelmed. Hussein was sent off to live in the household of his maternal uncle, Khairallah Talfah, for the first few years of his life.

The bonds that held the Al-Bu Nasir tribe together were strengthened by inter-marriage. Hussein's parents were cousins, and Subha eventually remarried to a man named Ibrahim al-Hassan, also her cousin, when Saddam was three. According to hearsay, the people of the village called Hussein's new stepfather "Hassan the liar" as they believed his adoption of the honorific title *hajj*, meaning one who has been to Mecca, was a lie. Once remarried, Subha brought her son back into her home where he was later joined by three more brothers.

Hussein lived with his family in a hut made from mud bricks. The family shared the one-room house and attached shed with their animals and had no electricity, running water, or lavatory. Hussein's stepfather did little to ease his family's poverty. Hussein later told stories of stealing chickens and eggs to feed his siblings; some even claim he was forced to steal by his stepfather. Hassan beat his stepson, although this was not uncommon amongst the clans of Al-Awja. What was uncommon was Hassan's loud public announcements that he didn't want his stepson, whom he called a "bastard" and "son of a dog," in his home. Hassan sent Hussein out to work the fields as a farmhand when he was around six years old, not allowing his stepson to begin his education.

Around the age of ten, Hussein left the harsh conditions in Al-Awja behind and moved to once again live with his uncle, Khairallah Talfah, in Tikrit. The Talfah family represented upward mobility and a refined existence that Hussein envied. Hussein later described escaping Hassan's hovel by leaving in the middle of the night and walking the distance to the Talfah home barefoot.

Khairallah was Subha's brother, a former second lieutenant in the Iraqi Army who had become a schoolteacher. He wore western clothes, and his son, Adnan, Saddam's cousin, attended school where he learned to read and write. Khairallah was a devout Sunni Muslim and had participated in the 1941 Rashid Ali Rebellion. In this rebellion, Nationalist Iraqi officers rose up against the pro-UK government of Iraq, the major colonial power in the region. The rebellion briefly established a pro-Nazi regime. Khairallah's politics would be a major influence in Hussein's life.

Chapter Two

From Peasant to Revolutionist

"Let them kill Nasser! What is Nasser but one among many? I am alive, and even if I die, all of you are Gamal Abdel Nasser!"

—Gamal Abdel Nasser, during an assassination attempt by the Muslim Brotherhood

Hussein started school around the age of ten and studied alongside students much younger than himself. Being poor and so far behind, he found the first few years of education challenging but progressed quickly. Teachers noted that the young boy's memory was so impressive it might have been photographic. In the early 1950s, Hussein moved with the Talfah family to Baghdad. Khairallah started a teaching position, and Hussein joined the nationalistic al-Karh Secondary School.

The family lived in a lower to middle-class suburb known as Al-Kharkh. In this mixed neighborhood full of new arrivals to Baghdad, Hussein had his first contact with Shia Muslims. Khairallah expressed prejudice towards the family's new Shia neighbors—an attitude

Hussein came to share. He was also influenced by Khairallah's opinion on recent events in Iraqi politics.

The late 1940s were a time of great political instability in Iraq. Governments often rose and fell, but the drama was largely confined to Baghdad, Basra, and Mosul. Most Iraqis were against British involvement in Iraq, but in January 1948, Shia Prime Minister Salih Jabr signed the Portsmouth Treaty. This treaty was like the 1930 agreement Iraq had with Great Britain and gave the foreign power the same colonial rights as before.

In May of 1948, Great Britain pulled out of Palestine, and the independent State of Israel was established. There were riots in the streets of Iraq that left scores dead. The Portsmouth Treaty was annulled, and the Iraqi Army joined other Arab armies to fight Israel in Palestine. Hussein had been insulated from these events in Tikrit, but as a student in Baghdad he couldn't help but feel the sea change. The power of the ruling elite was on shaky ground as street-level uprisings threatened to paralyze the government.

By the early 1950s, anti-government activism had taken over Hussein's life. Drawing on the politics of Gamal Abdel Nasser, the lieutenant colonel who overthrew the Egyptian government in 1952, Hussein became a leader of anti-government protests. President Jabr joined an anti-Communist alliance, the Baghdad Pact, in 1956. As part of this pact, Iraq offered support to Britain, France, and Israel instead of Egypt during the Suez Crisis. This move enraged the Iraqi people.

During protests, Hussein led gangs of thugs to intimidate local business owners. He also began carrying a gun which earned him the nickname *Abu Mussaddess,* "He of the Gun." Around 1959, after dropping out of law school, Hussein joined the revolutionary pan-Arab Ba'ath Party. In simple terms, the ideological aim of the Ba'ath was to join the Arab states of the Middle East together and use the power of their unity to expel foreign interference. Most members of the party were intellectuals or students from wealthy backgrounds. Like Stalin and his Communist revolutionaries in Russia, Hussein's humble origins set him apart; so much so that for the first few years of his involvement with the Ba'ath Party, he was not considered a member but a low-level supporter.

Gamal Abdel Nasser's successful coup and Egypt's victory in the Suez Crisis inspired nationalism in the Middle East. During the 1950s and 60s, the monarchies of Iraq, Egypt, and Libya collapsed, and the Arab world moved towards unity. In July 1958, after many unsuccessful attempts, the Iraqi Army overthrew the monarchy. Every unit of the Iraqi Army took part, and a committee of "Free Officers" stormed the royal palace. Brigadier Abd al-Karim Qasim and Colonel Abdul Salam Arif led the coup and murdered almost the entire royal family. Only the wife of the crown prince survived but was left for dead on a pile of corpses.

Hussein praised this bloody coup. He and more than a million Iraqis took to the streets to celebrate in a frenzy of looting and violence. Rioters attacked businesses and neighborhoods that represented the wealthiest class and murdered civilians. The death toll of this riotous revolution is unknown, but police arrested thousands of perpetrators. A mob seized Prince Abd al-Ilah's body, dragged it through the streets and hung it in front of the Ministry of Defence where it remained for two days. Prime Minister Nuri al-Said was also captured and killed. With his position assured, Qasim set up a Committee of Free Officers to conduct a Communist-style People's Court and try enemies of the people.

The Iraqi revolution had stirred neighboring countries. Arab unity posed a major threat to the West and its vested interest in its major oil-producing countries. A United Arab Republic that included Iraq could face off against the military might of Israel and completely destabilize the Middle East. Following the revolution, America sent forces to defend pro-West Lebanon. Statesmen from other nations, such as Canada, rushed to meet with the new Iraqi regime and find out what it was planning.

It soon became clear that Brigadier Qasim did not share Hussein's Ba'athist politics. A secret meeting between Qasim and Sir Michael Wright, the British ambassador in Iraq, took place days after the coup. Qasim made assurances to Wright about British involvement in Iraq that the Ba'athists would never have agreed to. The Committee of Free Officers split into two opposing factions. On one side was Qasim and his dream of an independent, inward-looking Iraq; on the other was the Ba'ath Party and its supporters who believed in Arab unity.

By the end of 1958, this ideological split had pushed Iraq to the brink of civil war. Surrounded by chaos and violence, Hussein put his talents to good use and organized his mob of petty criminals. He faced off against Qasim's own Communist-led militia, the Popular Resistance. Building roadblocks, invading homes, and attacking citizens, the Popular Resistance terrorized the people of Iraq. The brutality of the Popular Resistance's tactics made it easy for Ba'athists to recruit people to fight against them. Hussein took to the rebellion with gusto, and in November 1958, he was arrested and tried for murder. Due to a lack of evidence, he was only held for six months, but the incident enhanced his reputation as a man to be feared.

Chapter Three

An Assassin, a Ba'athist, and a Married Man

"Europe is as fearful of Islam today as she has been in the past. She now knows that the strength of Islam (which in the past expressed that of the Arabs) has been reborn and has appeared in a new form: Arab nationalism."

—Michel Aflaq

During the March 1959 Mosul Uprising, law and order in Iraq vanished. Pro-Nasser army officers, Arab nationalists, and Ba'athists clashed with Qasim and his Peace Partisans in an attempted coup. The coup was a failure and resulted in days of violence, the outcome of which still haunts Iraq. Hundreds died during the Mosul Uprising on both sides of the conflict.

As far as the Ba'athists and their UAR supporters were concerned, there was only one resolution: Qasim had to go. It's unclear whether Hussein volunteered for the role of gunman in the 1959 attempt to assassinate Qasim or whether he was ordered to take part. Either way, he joined a team of six other assassins on October 7, 1959 in a plot to murder to Qasim.

Qasim was a man of habit and drove through Al Rashid Street in central Baghdad at the same time every day. On the fated day in October, Hussein and his co-conspirators waited on Al Rashid Street until they saw their target and opened fire. The assassins shot Qasim twice, seriously injuring him and killing his driver. But the confusion caused by all seven men shooting at once meant two of the assassins were also shot. Abdel Wahab Ghoreiri died of his injuries, and Hussein was shot in the leg.

Hussein was still proud of his role in the botched assassination attempt. In July 1982, he escorted a *Time* magazine editor to Al Rashid Street to give a boastful account of his deed. Accounts from others present that day claim it was Hussein who shot prematurely and that he was responsible for Ghoreiri's death.

At the time, the would-be assassins believed they had killed Qasim. It was only upon their return to the Ba'athist headquarters that they learned Qasim had survived. So blind was the group's faith in their ability to assassinate Qasim, they had no backup plan in the event that he lived. The group had left Ghoreiri behind at the scene, so the Peace Partisans were able to deduce who else was involved.

Hussein escaped punishment by fleeing to Syria via Tikrit. With a bullet lodged in his leg, he made the journey across the Syrian desert to the border town of Abu Kamal. Syria was the spiritual home of Ba'athism, and Hussein was received by members of the party. He lived with Ba'athists in Damascus for three months.

During this time he recovered from his injury and befriended Michel Aflaq, the Christian Syrian co-founder of Ba'ath. Michel took a liking to Hussein and honored him with a full membership to the Ba'ath Party.

Michel sent Hussein, still in his early twenties, to Cairo where he attended Qasr al-Nil High School. From 1959 to 1961, he was a political exile, living on a small stipend provided by the UAR government and studying towards a law degree. Meanwhile, back in Iraq, Peace Partisans arrested anyone involved in the assassination attempt. Putting these young Ba'athist conspirators on trial was a bad move for Qasim. The men were unrepentant and argued that it was their duty as proud Iraqis to kill him. The men spoke with passion and criticized Qasim for his rejection of Arab nationalism and the benefits it could reap for the Iraqi people. Broadcast on the radio, the trials ended in death sentences for 17 of the 57 men on trial. The court sentenced Hussein to death in absentia.

In early 1962, while still in Cairo, Hussein celebrated his intended marriage to his cousin Sajida. Sajida's father Khairallah had promised Sajida to Hussein when they were both very young. It was an arranged marriage, and the betrothal was in line with Hussein's Bedouin heritage. Soon after, Hussein was elected as a member of the command of his branch of the Ba'ath Party.

On February 8, 1963, Iraqi Army units made a move to overthrow Qasim. Led by Hussein's cousin, General Ahmed Hassan al-Bakr, and his uncle, Khairallah, the coup lasted two days. Hundreds died during the two-day siege, and when Qasim finally surrendered he was put to death without a trial. Qasim had tried to spare lives by refusing to arm the Communist citizens who came to his defense and had led the first Iraqi regime to ever come to power without outside help. His recognition of Kurdish rights and respect for the poor gave him a lasting legacy as a beneficent leader.

A new government stepped into the void left by what became known as the Ramadan Revolution. Abdul Salam Arif became president of Iraq with the support of the coup leader and Hussein's cousin, Ahmed Hassan al-Bakr. Arif quickly installed his Ba'athist leaders in the cabinet. Together, Arif and al-Bakr merged their forces into the National Council for Revolutionary Command. The National Guard, the Ba'athist, and the Arab Nationalists who had fought alongside the Iraqi Army to topple Qasim were merged under the broad goal of "protecting the revolution." To achieve this goal, the National Guard purged Iraq of pro-Qasim and communist citizens. Death tolls vary, but it's thought that up to 35,000 people may have lost their lives following the Ramadan Revolution.

Hussein watched the coup and its aftermath from Cairo. Two weeks after Arif became president of Iraq, Hussein returned to Baghdad via Damascus. Michel Aflaq, who was now the head of the Ba'ath National Command, met with Hussein in Damascus. Hussein flew up the ranks to become a member of the President's Bureau, a vague position with duties that were open to interpretation.

Hussein got to work organizing the National Guard and punishing Communists for their perceived wrongdoings. No one knows if he carried out torture and executions at this time, but he did sanction killings. Hussein also took it upon himself to organize civilian cells of Ba'athists in the city and the villages. With this move, he extended his influence way beyond the National Guard. Now, Hussein was in control of the *fellaheen* (peasant) party members.

The Ba'ath Party's prominence in the Iraqi cabinet was short-lived as in November of 1963, President Arif conducted his own purge of Ba'athist leaders. Hussein remained in Iraq even though he was under threat of arrest and married Sajida who soon became pregnant. Major divisions within the Ba'ath Party threatened its future, and Hussein sidled closer to Michel Aflaq. At the 1964 Ba'ath Party conference in Damascus, Hussein was became the head of a temporary and secret Ba'ath Regional Command in Iraq.

As head of this new secret command, Hussein initiated a plan to assassinate President Arif. Arif's men discovered Hussein's plot to attack the Presidential Palace on September 5, 1964, and apprehended him. Arif sent Hussein to prison for two years, during which time he spent long spells in solitary confinement. Sajida visited her husband in the Public Security Building, bringing him books and news from home.

While Hussein was behind bars, Michel Aflaq made changes to the Ba'ath Party. Ahmed Hassan al-Bakr was promoted to secretary general of the Iraqi Branch of the

Ba'ath Party, and Hussein became his deputy. Then, around 1966, two developments rocked the Ba'ath Party. In Syria, a leftist faction broke away and ousted Aflaq from the Ba'ath National Command. Around the same time, Iraqi President Arif died in a helicopter crash, and his hopeless brother took over the presidency.

Under the advice of al-Bakr, who needed his deputy's help in handling these events, Hussein escaped from prison.

Chapter Four

Improving Iraq's Economy, Health Care, and Education

"Women make up one half of society. Our society will remain backward and in chains unless its women are liberated, enlightened and educated."

—Saddam Hussein

In July 1968, Hussein and his cousin al-Bakr finally overthrew President Abdul Rahman Arif, Salam Arif's successor. The bloodless coup had been on the cards for some time and was an ideological overthrow as well as a seizure of power. In Ba'ath meetings leading up to the coup, Hussein was open in his dream for Iraq. He said, "When we take over the government I'll turn this country into a Stalinist state."

Al-Bakr became president of Iraq, but surprisingly only six of the twenty-four new cabinet members were Ba'athists. As al-Bakr's right-hand man, Hussein assumed responsibility for the government's new expanded security service. The killings the Ba'athist National Guard had carried out in 1963 were still fresh in the Iraqi people's minds. To distinguish his new organization from its predecessor, Hussein named it the bureaucratic-sounding Office of General Relations. He installed himself in an office next door to the president. One of Hussein's first actions in his new role as head of the Office of General Relations was to remove the prime minister, al-Naif, from office. Afterward al-Bakr appointed himself as his own prime minister and minister for foreign affairs.

Throughout 1969, Hussein took control of many government departments and cemented his reputation as al-Bakr's *gada*, or tough guy. He recruited to the Office of General Relations from every sector of society but paid special attention to Shia men who had been left out of the Ba'ath Party. By the mid-1970s, there were more than 400,000 Ba'athists in Iraq.

From tiny cells in rural villages to big city branches, the Ba'ath Party penetrated all walks of life and eventually took over the Iraqi Army. Hussein enforced the rule that the Ba'ath was the only political party to which any member of the armed forces could belong, punishable by death. Hussein had complete control over the ever-expanding Popular Army, which was formed by civilian volunteers, and soon the Iraqi Army was under his thumb too. Now it would be almost impossible for a rebel faction to carry out a coup.

Iraq was a nation divided along social, religious, ethnic, and economic lines. Hussein got to work as early as 1970 to try to solve the Iraqi-Kurdish conflict. An olive branch was extended to the Kurdish people in the form of the 11 March 1970 Manifesto. The manifesto promised to share Iraqi wealth, halt interference in Kurdish affairs, and conduct a democratic election in Kurdistan. This last promise was notable as Hussein had no intention of conducting a democratic election in Iraq.

Hussein turned his attention to the modernization of the Iraqi economy. On June 1, 1972, he nationalized Iraqi oil. Later, Hussein named this date "Victory Day" and made his intentions crystal clear with the revolutionary slogan "Arab Oil for the Arabs." At the time, the majority of Iraq's oil sector was controlled by foreign interests. His strategy to increase Iraq's oil revenues contributed to the 1973 energy crisis when the cost of oil spiked all over the world. Ostensibly, Iraq was acting in support of the Arab members of the Organization of Petroleum Exporting Countries (OPEC). OPEC had imposed an embargo against the United States and other countries in retaliation for their support of Israel during the Yom Kippur War.

In 1974, Iraqi oil revenue rose to $5.7 billion from $575 million in 1972. Hussein channeled this money into innovative state welfare programs and improved the national infrastructure. Iraq established universal free schooling, a National Campaign for the Eradication of Illiteracy, support for families of soldiers, free hospitalization to all, and the most modernized public-health system in the Middle East. Though it seems incredible now, Hussein received an award from UNESCO for his part in transforming the Iraqi healthcare system. By 1980, 95% of all girls were attending school in Iraq, up from 34% in 1970. This led to a change in the status of women who were permitted to work in sectors that were previously denied to them. In 1977, women were allowed to join the armed forces in Iraq for the first time.

With sharp foresight, Hussein pushed forward the diversification of the Iraqi economy. Through a national infrastructure campaign, he brought mining and other heavy industries to new parts of the country. This generated jobs for hundreds of thousands of Iraqis. New roads connected Iraq's big cities and surrounding towns and villages. Within a few years Hussein brought electricity to every city in Iraq.

Iraq's transformation was astonishing, and every sector of society benefited from the new, modern Iraq. Suddenly there were new opportunities for the peasants who, before the 1970s, made up two-thirds of the Iraq population. Government expenditure for agricultural development doubled between 1974 and 1975, and Hussein mechanized agriculture on a large scale. Farmers became landowners and profited from their family's labor. For many, the rapid development pointed to a bright future filled with hope. All they had to do was pledge undying allegiance to Saddam Hussein.

To outsiders, Iraq's ambitious social and economic programs were almost too good to be true. While the positive effects of Hussein's unofficial early rule are undeniable, his actions weren't all good. Hussein was a student of Stalinist ideology and believed that terror and violence were the two main tools needed to control a society. To keep the monopoly on power he had so easily accrued, Hussein had to neutralize anyone who opposed the Ba'ath Party's ideology.

Chapter Five

The Ba'ath Party Purge

"The West need someone to tell the man who walks around with the biggest stick in the world, that that stick can't bring down God's house."

—Saddam Hussein

Hussein knew that to fulfill his role as the most powerful man in Iraq, he had to control Iraq's position within and outside of the Middle East. In 1972, he made an official alliance with the Soviet Union and signed a 15-year Treaty of Friendship and Cooperation. This move concerned the government of the United States that was deep into the Cold War.

Hussein's grandiose ambitions included making Iraq the leader of the Arab world. Over the course of many years, he promoted Iraqi leadership of all Arabs by espousing unity rather than dominance. In a scheme to bring agricultural workers into Iraq, Hussein relocated entire villages of Sunni Muslims from Egypt and Morocco. The Arab world made note of his generosity. Yet this scheme was financially unsustainable, and villagers returned to their home countries empty-handed at the outbreak of the Iran-Iraq War.

Before the war with Iran began, Hussein had to deal with the Kurdish rebellion of 1974. The relationship between the Iraqi government and the Kurds had been in decline since the 1970 Manifesto. A lack of goodwill on both sides had seen to it that the promises made in the manifesto had not been met. Tensions were also mounting between Iraq and Iran in the early 1970s due to a dispute over who owned the body of water that flowed between the two nations—the Shatt al-Arab.

With financial support from the Iran and U.S. governments and assistance from the CIA, Mustafa Barzani and his Kurdish rebels rose up. The rebellion overwhelmed the Iraqi Army and caused 60,000 civilian and military casualties. Months into the rebellion, the Iranian Shah met with Hussein. Hussein agreed to split the sovereignty of the Shatt al-Arab and to settle disputes over the two country's borders. Soon after, Iran withdrew its support for the Kurds, and the rebellion collapsed overnight.

In response to the rebellion, Hussein launched a harsh anti-Kurd policy in 1976. Ancient Kurd villages in the mountains were moved to the south of the country. This forced relocation destroyed their centuries-old way of life. Hussein also financed a Kurdish militia that he owned and operated and used to fight Kurdish dissidents. His discrimination of his own people extended to the Shia Muslim majority. In a chilling policy of ethnic discrimination, Hussein forced citizens to prove their genealogical heritage; if any citizen had Iranian lineage, even as much as five generations ago, he labeled them foreigners in Iraq. In a twisted move, Hussein offered any pure Iraqi a financial reward if they divorced a wife or husband who had Iranian heritage.

Finally, Hussein took steps to eradicate Communist influence in Iraq. It was already law that every member of the armed forces must be part of the Ba'ath Party, but in 1978, Hussein used this law to execute 19 men by also making the law retroactive. Anyone who had been a member of the Communist Party, even decades before, was under threat. The leadership of the Communist Party fled, and support from the Soviet Union was not forthcoming.

By 1976, al-Bakr had become a puppet president who signed whatever piece of paper Hussein put in front of him. Hussein had made himself general of the Iraqi armed forces, and the elderly al-Bakr relied on him to control all quarters of his government. Hussein was also the architect of Iraq's foreign policy and represented Iraq in all diplomatic situations. His power knew no bounds.

Together with his *mukhabarat* (secret police), General Security, and military intelligence, Hussein used citizens to spy on the rest of the population. During this era, kidnapping, assassination, and torture became everyday occurrences. This, combined with Hussein's clever use of propaganda, meant that it was only a matter of time before he would overthrow al-Bakr.

By 1979, everything was in place. The Iraqi Army, which had swelled to over 400,000 men, was commanded by Hussein's cousin, Adnan Khairallah. Hussein's half-brother, Barzan, commanded the mukhabarat. Another cousin, Sa'adoun Shaker, took care of the National Security Office, and Izzat Ibrahim al-Douri, Hussein's loyal follower, led the Popular Army. With all three groups opposing Hussein's leadership—the Kurds, the Shias, and the Communists—silenced and a new, huge middle class of Iraqis appeased by the fruits of his rule, Hussein was ready to seize the presidency.

In 1978, al-Bakr was pursuing treaties with Syria in the hope of uniting them as one country. Syria was also led by Ba'athists and a union between the countries would have clear benefits for them both. To strengthen the eastern front against Israel, Iraq announced that it was willing to send Iraqi troops to support Syria. But, al-Bakr's union with the Syrian President Hafez al-Assad threatened to curb Hussein's power. This was unacceptable, and Hussein set about destroying the possibility of a union.

Al-Bakr's attempt to flex his presidential power backfired, and on July 16, 1979, Hussein forced al-Bakr to resign. This move was backed by the governments of Jordan, Saudi Arabia, and the CIA, who also feared the consequences of a union between Syria and Iraq. That Hussein had to seek outside support before he made his move shows that he was not universally popular within the Ba'ath Party. Members of the Ba'ath Party leadership, some of whom had known Hussein for years, found his leadership problematic. These men advocated a democratic party election to decide who should step into al-Bakr's place.

Six days after forcing al-Bakr's resignation in what was essentially a bloodless coup, Hussein convened an assembly of the Revolutionary Command Council and hundreds of other Ba'ath Party leaders in Baghdad. For posterity, Hussein videotaped the event. Wearing his military uniform, Hussein took to the stage. He announced that the party had been betrayed by a Syrian plot and that the traitors were in the room. He then took a seat and the secretary general of the Command Council, Muhyi Abd al-Hussein Mashhadi, stood to make his confession. Mashhadi fingered members of the audience one by one. Armed guards dragged every man Mashhadi pointed to out of the hall. Hussein arrested 68 men during this meeting, their screams of innocence ignored.

Wiping tears from his eyes, Hussein read out a pre-prepared list of traitors and congratulated the 300 who remained in their seats. The unfortunate 68 were found guilty of treason in secret trials, and many of them were sentenced to execution. By August 1, 1979, the number of prominent Ba'ath Party members executed had reached the hundreds. Videotapes of what became known as "the purge" circulated throughout Iraq.

The remaining Ba'ath Party leaders could make no mistake. The fate of Iraq was in the hands of one man.

Chapter Six

The Iran-Iraq War

"Whoever tries to climb over our fence, we will try to climb over his house."

—Saddam Hussein

The Iran-Iraq War lasted eight years and was the longest war of the twentieth century. One of the inciting incidents that pushed the two countries into war was the Iranian Revolution of 1979. During the revolution, Ayatollah Khomeini's Islamic Republic overthrew a 2,500-year-old Persian monarchy. Khomeini was the leader of an Islamic fundamentalist movement in Iran and imposed a government founded on radical Islamic ideals. Such ideals were a threat to Hussein's secular rule, and he feared the emergence of a similar Islamic revolution in Iraq.

The relationship between Hussein and Khomeini had been hostile since the 1970s. Exiled from Iran in 1964, Khomeini lived in the holy Shia city of Najaf in Iraq. From here, Khomeini built up a strong following. Hussein expelled him in 1978 when he told Shia Muslims to rise up and topple Hussein. The expulsion backfired. Khomeini sought refuge in France where he was able to use the media to drum up support for his fundamentalist ideology all over the world.

Immediately after Khomeini took control of Iran, the sovereignty of the Shatt al-Arab waterway again sparked border conflicts. Publicly, Hussein maintained that the issue could be resolved by peaceful negotiations. Privately, he was planning an invasion. The United States government supported Iraq's invasion of Iran in retaliation for the 1979 Iran hostage crisis. During the crisis, 52 American diplomats and citizens were held against their will in the American embassy in Tehran, Iran for 444 days.

The U.S. alongside Kuwait, Saudi Arabia, and the rest of the Gulf States were on Hussein's side when he first invaded Iran in September of 1980. Viewed by the rest of the world as a more civilized and tolerant leader than Khomeini, Hussein became known as the "defender of the Arab world." Hussein's allies sent financial and military support for his invasion, in violation of international law.

The Iraqi Army attacked Tehran Airport before invading Khuzestan and declaring it a new province of Iraq. Khuzestan is rich in oil and a desirable addition to Iraqi territory. Initially, the Iraqi Army had the upper hand, but Iranian forces overwhelmed their troops with endless human wave attacks. The American-trained Iranian Air Force was superior to Iraq's and its ground-force was three times the size.

Nevertheless, by early October, the Iraqi Army had reached Abadan, Iran's second largest city. Iraq lay siege to Abadan but struggled to take control. Hussein was ineffective as a military strategist which led to failures on the battleground. Days into the fighting, Iraq was looking for ways to end the war. Hussein had hoped to mimic the 1967 Six-Day Arab-Israeli War and find a resolution through mediation. Yet it soon became clear that ending this conflict would be more difficult than starting it.

International allies of Iraq turned a blind eye to Hussein's use of chemical weapons against Iran and Kurdish separatists. The weapons used technology developed in the United States and materials from West Germany. The U.S. also shared intelligence with Hussein, giving him access to satellite photos of Iranian deployments. Other allies—the Soviet Union, France, and China—supplied Iraq with arms for the duration of the eight-year war. The United Nations Security Council, however, made repeated calls for a ceasefire.

Chapter Seven

A War with No Victor

"The great duel, the mother of all battles has begun. . . . The dawn of victory nears as this great showdown begins!"

—Saddam Hussein

Before the Iran-Iraq War, the Soviet Union supplied most of Iraq's weapons. Hussein recognized that his country's reliance on a foreign power for military hardware left him vulnerable. Back in 1970, Moscow had already tried to apply political pressure by withholding arms. In the mid-1970s, Hussein began to skim 5% of all Iraqi oil income. He set this money aside in a Swiss bank account and referred to it as the Fund for Strategic Development.

Both the Soviet Union and the West (excluding France) declared an embargo on supplying arms to Iran and Iraq when the war began. Hussein turned to Egypt which agreed to help him maintain his existing Russian-made military hardware. Jordan also agreed to supply Iraq with arms, which gave other countries an opportunity to get around the embargo. Italy sold arms to Iraq via Jordan as did South Africa. Soon, Saudi Arabia was providing Iraq with military assistance, and Kuwait followed suit.

Before long, Iran was forced to accept help from its religious foe, Israel. The United States supplied Israel with the majority of its arms. Supply contracts stipulated that the arms manufacturing country must approve the transfer of arms to another country. The U.S. gave approval and began indirectly supplying arms to Iran. The U.S. used Iraq's preoccupation with Iran to assist Israel in destroying the atomic reactor Hussein had built in Osirak. Hussein eventually found out about America's treachery and was furious.

As the war dragged on, conditions in Iraq deteriorated. The government operated independently of all legal constraints. Hussein's security apparatus was responsible for the kidnap and murder of hundreds of civilians, and Hussein routinely executed his own generals and cabinet members. On one notorious occasion, he executed his minister for health, Riyadh Ibrahim, in the middle of a cabinet meeting.

Throughout the war, Hussein expanded his unconventional chemical, biological, and atomic weapons program. He replaced the French nuclear reactor which Israel had destroyed and pushed his scientists to develop new weapons. On March 16, 1988, Hussein used chemical weapons to invade the Kurdish town of Halabja. The Iraqis attacked with a mix of mustard gas and nerve agents killing more than 5,000 civilians and injuring 10,000 more.

At the time, Hussein maintained that Iran carried out the attack, a claim repeated in the U.S. press. Iran was weakened by the criminal attack on Halabja. Unnerved by America's duplicity and in fear of more chemical attacks on their cities, Iran's northern front collapsed. Khomeini began referring to the United States as the "Great Satan."

On July 18, 1988, Khomeini accepted the UN Security Council's Resolution 598 to end the war. The borders of Iran and Iraq were largely unchanged, but their economies were shattered. An estimated 360,000 Iraqi and Iranian citizens had been killed and 700,000 more injured in a war that cost over $600 billion. But according to Hussein, he was victorious.

Chapter Eight

The Gulf War

"Everyone can cause harm according to their ability and their size. We cannot come all the way to you in the United States, but individual Arabs may reach you."

—Saddam Hussein

After eight years of brutal warfare, the Iraqi people had little to celebrate. International friends had become foes when the world's attention shifted to Hussein's use of chemical weapons and human rights abuses. The price of oil had plummeted, and Iraq could not afford to pay its debts and meet the country's financial needs. Hussein also had a post-war army of over a million men he was unable to compensate.

To create a solid social foundation from which he could fight growing Shia radicalism in Iraq, Hussein needed cash. He asked Kuwait to waive the $30 billion of debt Iraq had accumulated during the war, but Kuwait refused. Together Iraq and Kuwait were in control of around one-fifth of the world's oil reserves. However, Kuwait's population was far lower than Iraq's, and it was able to pump huge amounts of oil while keeping the price low. Only by minimizing Kuwait's production could Hussein raise Iraqi oil prices.

Hussein pushed a disagreement over debt and oil production into dangerous territory when he reminded the Iraqi people that Kuwait was once a part of Iraq. Iraqi nationalists had been desperate to invade Kuwait for the last 50 years. Hussein capitalized on this idea as a way of uniting a society divided on almost everything else. In his first move, Hussein contested the border between Iraq and Kuwait. Next, he accused Kuwait of drilling oil from wells that were technically within Iraq. Then Hussein stationed Iraqi troops at the Kuwait border.

Hussein's intentions were becoming clear, but he was receiving confused intelligence about how the U.S. would react if he invaded Kuwait. At the time Iraq was the third largest recipient of American aid. It was in President Reagan's best interests to keep the U.S. and Iraq on friendly terms, so he sent an ambassador to meet with Hussein.

On July 25, 1990, American ambassador to Iraq, April Glaspie, met with Hussein to discuss a slew of recent threats. A few months earlier, Hussein had threatened to destroy half of Israel with chemical weapons if it moved against Iraq. He also attacked the U.S. for its support for Israel and made threats against Kuwait and the United Arab Emirates. As far as Hussein was concerned, America was working with other Arab rulers to undermine Iraq and thwart efforts to rebuild his country.

During the meeting, Glaspie stressed that the United States had no opinion on Arab-Arab conflicts. She asked, in the spirit of friendship, what Hussein's intentions were at the Kuwait border. Hussein's rhetoric was threatening;

he said, "If you use pressure, we will deploy pressure and force. We know that you can harm us although we do not threaten you. But we too can harm you. Everyone can cause harm according to their ability and their size. We cannot come all the way to you in the United States, but individual Arabs may reach you."

Iraq invaded Kuwait on August 2, 1990, instigating an international crisis that forced the most invested nations to act. The Soviet Union immediately offered Hussein arms, aid, and military expertise. The United States condemned Hussein's actions and enforced immediate economic sanctions against Iraq.

In a swift and efficient operation, Iraqi armor and paratroops occupied Kuwait in four hours. Kuwait's royal family escaped by following a plan set up with American support. Less than a week after the invasion, Hussein announced a merger of the two countries, and Kuwait became the 19th governorate of Iraq.

A UN coalition of 35 nations led by the United States entered Kuwait in February 1991. Now Hussein was able to use his still impressive Iraqi military machine against some of the nations that had paid for it. The West's involvement in what became known as the Gulf War cited a flagrant violation of international law as its motivation. However, coalition nations were also invested in Middle Eastern politics because peace helped keep global oil prices stable. Great Britain, in particular, benefited from its investments in Kuwait. Some economists feared that war in the Middle East could threaten the stability of the entire global economy.

U.S. operations leading up to the Gulf War were known as Operation Desert Shield while the combat phase was Operation Desert Storm. The United States and Soviet Union worked with the UN Security Council to give Hussein a deadline for leaving Kuwait. Complicated diplomatic machinations between the coalition, Hussein, and Arab leaders meant alliances and settlements changed by the hour. Hussein did not act on the Security Council's deadline, and the coalition launched around-the-clock missile and aerial attacks on Iraq. A ground force then entered Kuwait, led by British and American infantry divisions, and occupied the southern part of Iraq.

The Iraqi Army, although the largest and best-equipped army in the Middle East at the time, was unable to compete with the coalition forces. President Bush ordered a cease-fire on February 28, 1991, but not before perpetrating a massacre of Iraqi civilians and military personnel at Mittlah Ridge. Hussein signed a surrender agreement on March 3, 1991. Two days later the Shia population of southern Iraq rose up in rebellion against Hussein. Within weeks, 60% of Iraq was in rebel hands.

Chapter Nine

Rise of Islamic Fundamentalism

"Our children should be taught to beware of everything
foreign and not to disclose any state or party secrets to
foreigners . . . for foreigners are eyes for their countries, and
some of them are counterrevolutionary instruments [in the
hands of imperialism]."

—Saddam Hussein

An estimated 10-12,000 Iraqis died in combat during the Gulf War. A further 10,000 people were injured. Despite the Iraqi death toll and UN trade sanctions that continued long after the war ended, Hussein again claimed victory. His insistence, despite all evidence to the contrary, that his Kuwait campaign had been a success intensified the rebellion against him.

What became known as the 1991 *intifada* was a Shia and Kurdish uprising in Iraq. The United States refused to assist Iraqi rebels fighting against Hussein, hoping to slow the spread of Islamic fundamentalism. Iran also declined to support the rebels, fearing the U.S. would step in and take matters into their own hands. Egypt took a more direct approach and warned the U.S. to stay out of what became a civil war.

Hussein gave shoot-to-kill orders "to crush the centers of treason and perfidy." Free to use every member of the Iraqi Special Forces and Popular Army, Hussein systematically executed the rebels. Yet it wasn't until popular opinion turned against the rebels that the intifada truly failed. The rebels tortured, decapitated, and dismembered hundreds of people. This brutality united Sunni Muslims, the Iraqi Army, and ordinary civilians against them. By the first week of April 1991, the south of Iraq was back in Hussein's hands, and an estimated 50,000 to 300,000 southern Iraqis were dead.

Hussein then turned his attention to the north and invaded Kurdistan. Within two weeks, he had reconquered rebel-held areas and ordered the mass murder of Kurds in the region. The Kurdish leader appealed to the West for help. The prime minister of Great Britain, John Major, made a personal plea to President Bush to stop the killing.

The UN passed Resolution 687 which, among other things, ordered a cessation of the killing of the indigenous people of Iraq. This was followed by France, the United States, and Great Britain's Operation Provide Comfort which promised to protect the Kurdish people. Approximately 100,000 Kurdish people died, and more than 2 million were displaced before the West stepped in and put a stop to the genocide.

The Gulf War and resulting intifada had shattered the Iraqi military. As part of the ceasefire agreement, the UN forced Iraq to dismantle its germ and chemical weapons program. Hussein was to allow UN inspectors into Iraq to ensure that these terms were being met. But sanctions placed on Iraq by the UN when Hussein invaded Kuwait remained in place. President Bush stated that the sanctions would remain until Hussein was removed, another call to arms for rebels inside Iraq to stage a coup. The former CIA case officer assigned to the Middle East, Robert Baer, stated that during the "decade-long effort to encourage a military coup in Iraq," he eventually tried to assassinate Hussein in 1995. Another significant outcome from keeping the sanctions in place was that they blocked the export of oil, Iraq's main source of revenue.

The relationship between Iraq and the United States was hostile and erupted in violence when the U.S. accused Iraq of violating no-fly zone agreements. On June 26, 1993, the United States launched a missile attack on Iraq's military intelligence headquarters in Baghdad. The U.S. repeatedly accused Iraq of violating the terms of the Gulf War ceasefire and being in possession of weapons of mass destruction. Accusation turned into action in December of 1998 when American and British forces launched intensive missile strikes on Iraq.

Despite international protest, the United States and Great Britain unleashed a four-day bombing campaign on Iraq between the 16th and 19th of December 1998. This campaign had no specific goal, other than to punish Hussein in a united show of strength. On December 18, an attack on an oil refinery in Basra killed dozens of Iraqi civilians. The lives of ordinary Iraqi people were at risk, but this was nothing new.

Sanctions imposed on Iraq by the UN led to many Iraqi deaths during the late 90s. The economy in Iraq was so unstable and its people so poor that Hussein eventually accepted the terms of an Oil-for-Food Programme. Established in 1995 by the UN, this programme allowed Hussein to sell oil on the international market in exchange for food, medicine, and other humanitarian items.

Over the next two years, the United States and Great Britain continued to bomb Iraq, exacerbating the humanitarian crisis. In 2002, the EU stepped in with a resolution sponsored by the Commission for Human Rights. The resolution accused Hussein of committing atrocious violations of human rights and demanded that he put a stop to "summary and arbitrary executions, including political killings and the continuing prison cleansing, the use of rape as a political tool and all enforced and involuntary disappearances."

Hussein was indeed committing grave violations of international human rights laws. Yet a large percentage of the starving population of Iraq still supported him. One Iraqi observer noted that "people forgot about Saddam's record and concentrated on America. . . . Saddam Hussein might be wrong, but it is not America who should correct him."

Hussein garnered support from various groups in the Arab world for standing up to the United States. Re-branding himself as a devout Muslim, Hussein returned to the rhetoric of his early Ba'athist days. Promoting Arab unity and self-sufficiency, he reintroduced elements of *sharia* law to Iraq. He also added the phrase "Allahu akbar" (God is great) to the Iraqi flag and commissioned the writing of a Blood Qur'an using his own blood. Islamic fundamentalism was ascending.

Chapter Ten

U.S. Invasion and Hussein's Execution

"There is no god but God and Muhammed [is His prophet]."

—Saddam Hussein's last words

On September 11, 2001, a group of 19 men identifying as part of the Islamic extremist group al-Qaeda carried out terror attacks on the United States. The group hijacked four airplanes. They flew two airplanes into the twin towers of the World Trade Center in New York City and one into the Pentagon outside of Washington D.C. Almost 3,000 people were killed in the attacks. Fifteen of the nineteen perpetrators were citizens of Saudi Arabia, two were from the United Arab Emirates, one was Egyptian, and one was Lebanese. The rise of Islamic extremism in the Middle East became the rest of the world's primary concern.

In November 2002, the UN passed Security Council Resolution 1441. This resolution demanded that Iraq resume cooperation with the UN and International Atomic Energy Agency (IAEA). The world wanted to inspect Iraq's nuclear weaponry and confirm or deny its possession of weapons of mass destruction (WMDs). Under pressure, Hussein agreed to the inspections which were carried out by Hans Blix, UN chief weapons inspector.

Following this inspection, the Iraqi government provided the UN with a 12,000-page weapons declaration. This document was a complete inventory of Iraq's chemical, biological, nuclear, and missile weaponry. Blix reported finding no weapons of mass destruction in Iraq. Yet the United States and Great Britain expressed concern that Iraq's weapons declaration was incomplete. On February 14, 2002, Blix reported to the UN again, stating that Iraq must do more to prove it has no WMDs. Blix warned that the inspectors needed more time to work with the Iraqi government and come to a resolution.

As far as the United States and Great Britain were concerned, time had run out for Saddam Hussein. The "no WMD" findings of Blix's inspections were not enough to quell anti-Iraq sentiment building in the United States and Great Britain. Intelligence from Russia in late 2001 indicated that Hussein was preparing terrorist attacks against the US.

On January 29, 2002, President George W. Bush made his stance clear naming Iraq, along with Iran and North Korea, as the "axis of evil." The prime minister of Great Britain, Tony Blair, shared President Bush's sentiments. Blair told Bush that he would support the U.S. in any attempt to overthrow Hussein, with or without UN approval. Bush used his 2003 State of the Union address to announce the start of Operation Iraqi Freedom, promising to liberate the Iraqi people.

The invasion of Iraq began on March 20, 2003, and by April 9, American forces had taken control of Baghdad. In a symbolic act, U.S. Marines assisted Iraqi civilians to topple a 12-meter statue of Hussein located at Firdos Square. Photographs of the falling statue made front page news all over the world, symbolizing the fall of Saddam Hussein's dictatorship. It took three weeks for coalition forces to take control of Iraq, and President Bush declared victory on May 2, 2003.

The last video of Hussein appearing in public in Iraq was shot in the suburbs of Baghdad soon after the American invasion. Following that, he disappeared. Hussein retreated into hiding, but his family kept up their defense of his regime. On July 22, 2003, U.S. soldiers raided a villa in the northern Iraqi city of Mosul. Living in the villa were Hussein's two sons, Uday and Qusay, and his 14-year old grandson, Mustafa. All three were killed in the course of a three-hour long gunfight.

The United States released a list of the 55 most-wanted members of the Iraqi regime with Saddam Hussein at number one. The manhunt for the former dictator intensified until, on December 13, 2003, Hussein was finally captured. He was hiding in a hole in the ground in ad-Dawr, near Tikrit. Creating a spectacular circle out of the narrative of his life, Hussein had returned to the humble farmland in which he grew up. He did not resist arrest, and soldiers at the scene said he resembled "a man resigned to his fate." Hussein was taken to the American base near Baghdad where, according to U.S. officials, he was found to be in good health.

By January of 2005, the Iraqi people had elected a new 275-member Iraqi National Assembly. A new Iraqi constitution was drawn up and ratified in October 2005 and in the same month, Hussein went to trial for crimes against the Iraqi people.

The first trial of Saddam Hussein centered around a specific event that occurred in the Shia Muslim town of Dujail in 1982. The charges leveled against Hussein included premeditated murder, imprisonment, deprivation of physical movement, forced deportation, and torture. He was accused of murdering 148 people, illegally arresting 399 people, and torturing women and children. A second trial against Hussein began in August 2006 in which he was tried on genocide charges. Operation Anfal, a genocidal campaign that lasted throughout the 1980s, claimed the lives of an estimated 100,000 Kurdish people.

Hussein was found guilty of crimes against humanity on November 5, 2005 and sentenced to death. Although he would have preferred death by firing squad, Hussein was executed by hanging on December 30, 2006. The next day he was buried at his birthplace of Al-Awja in the Tikrit region, Iraq. It is thought that Hussein's body has since been removed from his tomb and stored in a secret location to protect it from desecration.

Conclusion

The Iraq War did not end when President Bush declared victory on May 2, 2003. Today, Iraq remains a country ravaged by combat where conflict affects every province from north to south and east to west. The American-led coalition of the 2003 invasion defeated the military forces of Iraq, but dozens of volatile militant groups emerged in its wake. A state of constant guerrilla war is Iraq's new normal.

Saddam Hussein led a Ba'athist regime that was ultra-violent and oppressed the human rights of the people of Iraq. That much is undeniable. But what replaced his regime in Iraq was likely worse. Before 2003, al-Qaeda was practically non-existent in Iraq. The group was perceived as a threat within Ba'athist Iraq and suppressed by Hussein's government. President Bush's War on Terror had the paradoxical effect of creating the conditions for groups like al-Qaeda and ISIL/ISIS to flourish.

Global recruitment to these groups increased dramatically following the American invasion. The power vacuum Saddam Hussein left behind was filled with brand new warlords. Anti-Shia and anti-Sunni sectarianism violently shakes the foundations of Iraq to this day. A study published by *The Lancet* in 2006 showed that in the first three years of the U.S. invasion, approximately 655,000 Iraqis were killed. The death toll keeps rising.

A conservative estimate puts the number of Iraqis killed by Hussein's security services in purges and genocide at 250,000. Yet there were brief moments of prosperity. While still vice-president in the 1970s, Saddam orchestrated a nationwide literacy campaign. As part of this campaign, hundreds of thousands of illiterate Iraqis learned to read. However, it is not literacy that threatens a dictatorship but what the public is reading—and dictators are always censors. Hussein established one of the best public health systems in the Middle East but filled its hospitals with Iraqi citizens. Tyrants have a tendency to give with one hand and take away with the other.

It's rarely mentioned now but Saddam Hussein was a charismatic man and he rose to power using a formidable mixture of charm and threat. His ability to hide his true intentions was his greatest skill. His son Uday was once quoted as saying, "My father's right shirt pocket doesn't know what is in his left shirt pocket."

Once Hussein became the president of Iraq, the positive changes he had made became a distant memory. As president, Hussein's ambitions turned to conquest and sacrificing his own people to achieve his ends never troubled him. Hussein achieved absolute power, but maintaining that power, fighting off the constant threat of a coup or foreign invasion, corrupted him.